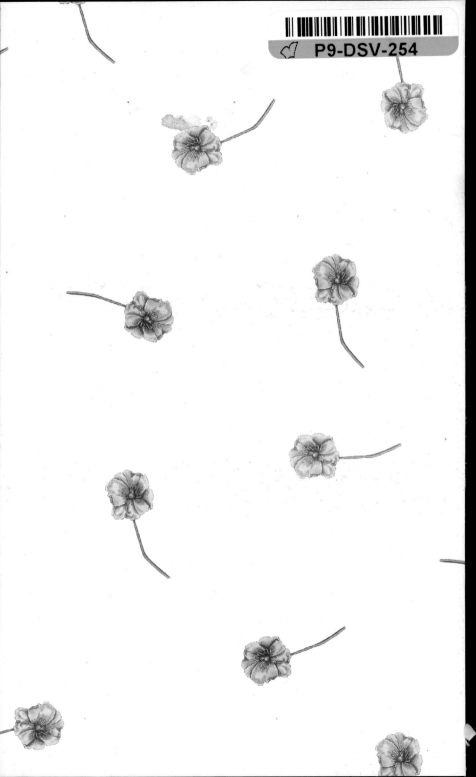

The Laughing Dove
and other Poems

The Laughing Dove
and other Poems

Vernon RL Head

STAGING
POST
The Stories We Tell

First published by Staging Post in 2015

10 Orange Street
Sunnyside
Auckland Park 2092
South Africa
+2711 628 3200
www.jacana.co.za

ISBN 978-0-9946677-8-6

Cover design by publicide
Set in Sabon 11/16pt
Printed and bound by ABC Press, Cape Town
Job no. 002600

DEDICATED TO:

BirdLife South Africa

CONTENTS

OLD PEOPLE

have shouted time at me like a warning;
and a day has changed into an exquisite place:
a room of wilderness searching for faces
that see the fecund clock of smiles.

His Name is Bigshow

He lives in a street of crushed diamonds

Straight

Steep

Long

Linked

Stretched like a line of lies

When the rain comes
It takes Table Mountain to the Ocean in fast cars
Windscreens are his currency
Prisons for clouds
Purple pigeons follow like children and
Butterflies flap in search of flowers in bougainvillea hair
His pockets are caves for bees
When sleeping, his clothes squeak like dawn-mice
And then he polishes

Once, there was a little stream bent softly in green clicks. All floated in a sun of bubbles. Frogs glowed as busy pebbles. Warm earth shaped a gentle way for black ducks, brown francolins and red robins to hop like traffic down to the Bay:

Kloof Street

Sparkling

Uncut in jewels.

CERES ORCHARD

Rows of toys
Hold lines like pages
Peeling oranges into little hands
Gently wet on a sticky mist
Stretching the day down to the Dam
Reeds blinking feathers
Dusting sleep from sentences
In a sky of leaves and laughter
Bounced by butterflies
And tickled bees

Mud was toes then
Shade was a long place of stories
Sweet, yellow flowers twirled
In a kaleidoscope of collected things
Among a carnival of words

And a new, white bird plopped onto the Dam
Of rippled moments
Bronzed by dusk
Cast hard like memory

Scaring everything

HOME

(For Kathleen)

The garden bird –
like the bee and the moth –
belongs to moments
passing through holes
in still days,
and little
gaps
in the middle of nights;
unfenced,
riding irrelevant
lines
between sanctuaries.

The garden bird –
like the fish and the frog –
splashes
over
walls (and nets)
and frames:
frilly edges of froth
linking seas and ponds,
coming and going
in shores of perception.

Green and blue
reflection:
the cave,
once flickering
as a door,
carved below moons
in moods of
ancient sticks
before the world of bricks and books and borders.
Our lives
are patterned in
temporariness:
a language of languages,
muddled to speak
of a texturing wind
and faraway sunsets
behind very high, old hills.

One day
the clouds might
drop singing birds
to be heard in between every home,
just in time for our humanity:
spectacularly vast and visited,
stretched, finger-tipped and toed
to touch
dependently at a private
new body:
the gentle,
special arrangement:
the shadows of suburban flutterings,
warm
between wings.

THE END

March Lily of the lawn,
In blushing dews,
Pink-pushed, up like a fist of
Bending bugles reaching for sound;
Lips with a link to the ground.

I drove my father to the hospital in a slow emergency,
Ageing the end of summer:
An early siren of dawn:
Fire Lily of the Lawn.

Alone on the verge of memories,
On a road of black,
Sifting the air near
The Flower of Fear, we went.

And a distant chimney smoked of bones and skin,
Curling birds in greys from within.

BRINK

His wall of books now just a wall
A spine less than a spine
A leaf less than a leaf
Great tree of cracks fluttering in vacant bits of
    vertebrae
Gilded bones now embossed on clouds
All the colours of our world only packed and painted
In tight temporariness
All the shelves waiting for dust
Hands flat to the light
Praying as stiff coffins for paper

BEFORE PROSE

Writing poems at dawn is
finding a clear pool on a forest stream,
watching water grant the sky to the clouds,
holding little bits of birds and mirrored bees,
dancing on the edge of stories and trees,
lovely, and alone, flickering in the beginning of things.

Writing poems at dawn is
a place to swim,
dipped on the dreams that ripple foundling shapes,
echoes from the sun;
all cut from the sides of leaves, from puzzles, and
　　from memories.

Writing poems at dawn is
freshly wet in new complications:
the glistening of new babies.

ON THE DEATH OF A BIRDWATCHER

(For Margot Chamberlain)

Oceans never end in crashing waves,
they begin as quiet shores
at the pause before oars.

There is something that happens on the coast.
Do not see the sea, instead smell where it ends and,
before long,
you will be in the green country
of trees and whales.

At the horizon of raining fish and seabirds
water holds the air of leaves,
all wet in waves of
living things.
Trees will float in pollen.
Fish will fly among roots and sails;
and the blades of the plough will reflect the light
of one trillion empty seashells:
never ending rafts pearled in
connectedness.

KAROO THORN

Tiny clouds of air hold
The wind in the shade of places
Like antelopes herded by fear.
Green against blue and white,
Leaves profit from the spear.
Between the softness is the snake,
Sharp of words,
Hard of warnings.

LIGHTED AVENUES

Some lighted houses hold golden paths
In the rain like snakes
Sharply whipped from holes.

Flickering television sets
Vomit onto plastic lawns near
Little, luminous dogs squatting out diamonds.

Vast trees glow soap operas.
Sprinklers hiss lies.
Swimming pools slam polished attentions at the skies.

Dragonflies shine afloat in queues
Near ornate spigots crammed with dead pigeons,
And festivals of spouting feathers and faux feelings
    make
Waterfalls of pain.

High walls of lost butterflies flap concussed
Against the sharp, sparkling suburb of shame.

SPELLING FACES

(For Mom and Arch)

Eyelids of night
Hang heavy on our cliff of wings.
High talkings of hard things
Sprinkle conversations of spelling faces.
And in the blink of an eye,
The temporariness of places,
The misunderstandings and explanations,
And a dawn of races.
So many valleys and trees and rocks
Crack in the green light
Of a soft Karoo:
'*Ko-Ka Tsara, Ko-Ka Tsara*'.
The dove-heat, the family, the dust-feet.
A *kloof* to a new morning of letters.

WITWATERSRAND

Mine dumps are the wheels of rust.
Yellow-edged dams: dead.
And a red shopping centre plumes
Like violence fed.
Roads rip cars
In cells of blood,
And all is a pus of people
Wounding tomorrow
For the birds.
Long gone is that high, feathered peak.

LAUGHING DOVE

Bruised air sat in the colours of pain.
Thoughts tapped a shadow of rain.
And, then a fragile nod of neck,
Because a motorbike came.
The pause (at traffic lights),
the teetering,
the frame.

Paved in lonely cracks, a grid of trees and walls and
    clouds burnt
a concrete net of corridors
for lonely walkers and wheels.
There, it cried: this place – in between – of fumes
    and little, laughing birds.

FRIED FRUIT BAT

Long on the wires now,
Stilled, hard and stranded electrically.
On the lines of light,
Where obligations cooked it
In volts of night.
The sun came on the fruit bat:
Black leaf of Sri Lanka.
Hard, dead as a flag
Of instinct and glistening flies.

We should live upside down,
Because when we die we will see the future:
A hole:
Angled black for the stiff;
Dried in the winds
Of owls and air.

AIRLINER

Clouds seen from above are irrelevantly bright,
But below, blue ideas move deep shades
On the green fields of Johannesburg.
Soft moments of ground:
Opportunities for cool thought and
Delicious, lost wanderings.
No more flights for me,
Time to walk.

POLITICS IN PARLIAMENT

The Tree near the window makes a shadowed wall
High leaves are birds
Low leaves fall
A hole frames glass
Hard, open to our sky,
Light comes and goes in green (and red),
And – by the by – inside
A President speaks,
But these buildings stand on rusting leaves

(Selected for the *2014 Sol Plaatje European Union
Poetry Anthology*)

THE SEARCH FOR AFRICAN

The born and the brain are torn.
A tree bends into white thorn.
Footprints fill rows for words and
Sentences hunt in transmutation
On lands like the scraping toes of birds.
Clouds cast memories, inking rivers.
Caves move in lungs:
Fleshy leaved of shaded ponderings,
dripping invention, earthed and birthed.

Tattoo Rock.
Art of fact.

The born and the brain are torn;
Africa is a nest of thorn.

CAPE TOWN
(For Pola Jocum)

Is land
He-ad land
Sea land
Land-ed

Cliff
Point
Nelson
Coon

Wine
Class
Jazz
Tune

Sugar birds in a tree
Gull birds bend the sea
Sun birds and money
Wind birds for free

Moon

No butterflies on the moon

Blackish
Flighted around no sound
Reflecting memories
Flapping and folding
A temporary Solitaire
Like a chrysalis found
In tomorrow
Growing silvery

A place
Winged in the turn of dreams
Bright to a faded
Flowerless face
Fractured on a crease
Of yesterday

No butterflies on the moon

WILDERNESS

(For Dr Phoebe Barnard and SANBI)

A palm tree in the fynbos

A garden
A new shape of shade
Like a cutting blade

A palm tree in the fynbos

Cape Town becoming Cairo
Fresh desert near cold sea
Latitude on the shifting degree

A palm tree in the fynbos

Sunny flowers cracking ice
Petals scattered like dice
Blizzards of out-of-place Chinese rice

A palm tree in the fynbos

New dusts that compete
New rain for traded heat

New space for foreign languages of feet
A palm tree in the fynbos

Plastic orchid in a vase
Bobbing waterless
Of wilderness
In waste

MASTERPIECE

(In memory of Prof. Roelof Uytenbogaardt)

On the concrete edge
Are hard clouds
Bent away from people.

Shy in shadows,
Windowed moods played privately
Like children,
Painting with the rain:
Dripping greetings and stains
for sleeping *bergies*.

His walls held light
And the most aerial lightness.
His sketches came strong like cliffs.
His hands reached long like rivers.
His eyes were kind, like cities can be.

Money came and
Glass turned into
Curving Ray-Bans
Reflecting stares of
Vacancy.

That building was our place to see
A street – at last – a vision:
The valleys of villages;
The paths of peoples.

A *mossie's* nest curled of art.

Paper Words

Africa to America sways in new slaves.
A trade of words:
the keyboard of shackled fingers and minds.
And the white arc of iCloud pulls new birds down to
    new cages,
calling the ring-a-ding-ding of the fibre-optic bridge.

Soft links of rain stain a blotting sea,
stretched into blurred paper,
smashed like pieces of petrified wood.

We long for the old place
that sheltered the slow:
the gorgeous isolation of footpaths and dusty tracks:
the storytimes once filled with considerations and
    families that
gave seeing eyes to eyes.
In that spit of men (and women)
came the words of African highs.

The knitting of beads and wild birdsong are gone.
Just a tide of waves now,
rolling in a light of sparkling pixels.

ANNE'S OVERBERG

(In memory of Anne Gray)

We drive in the edge of change: the road of birds.

On pollen air the field is a
Splash of hills:
green, yellow, green, yellow, green.
Swaying black kelp lines reach
high on the great wave of Overberg.
Popping dams make holes on a swell that
farms fences, bending above into a sea anemone.
Nearby the tongues of sheep
wiggle like fish.

A little carcass of squashed feathers
tinkles with foreign weeds and waste at the verge,
and a cracked beak leaks blood.
Her land has lost a memory of a distant route:
a road between roads.

Tomorrow there will be no wave for the wild aloe,
no meadow for the whale,
no tide,
just flood.

Rock

(For Peter Sullivan)

Of the sparkling sand
Of the wobbling sea
Of the bouncing wind
Of the shining wave
Of the shifting ground
Of the pushing hill
Of the pulling valley
Of the settling soil
Of the wetting sky
Of the stretching tree
Of the folding flower
Of the bending river
Of the stillness of a quiet lake
Of the singing bird
Come rocks

Of the crying, little boys
Of the helplessness of men
Of the urine on stained feet
Of the buried and dry lands
Of the burning buildings
Of the waste-plastic and waste-tyres
Of the screaming crowds

Of the shitting on streets
Of the fighting and bombs
Of the rubble and smoke
Of the holes in all walls
Of the loudness of the BBC
Of the hospitals and red beds
Of the tunnels under Gaza
Come rocks

BEES

A bee
is a bit of a thing,
holding petals
in the yellow sky
with thoughts of a song.
Shining, sticky nets
drip trees:
a mesh of shouts
and turns.
So sweetly cast,
metallic,
shaped alone
in gregariousness.
Apart and together,
aired,
for busy birds.
Our world reflecting
the rolling pond of
hardening syrup, and
a bee: meadow; flock of swallows; forest tips.
All one.
Aglow.

COAST HOUSE

A small farmhouse of salt
opens in sleep,
shutterless and
floating like a
cliff:
ocean-white in hard walls, high walls, soft walls
grainy rhythms of night in flight afloat.
All in the rise and the fall of the Bay,
Long eaves – the oars – pull breath, and
sails bend doors and the doorway.

Alone,
the current glows (and bobs) in wheat.
Within a field plops a pond:
holed of stars glittering in fishish frogs.

The warm light of lungs,
softly hums on thatch,
and a mattress moves.
Coffee and the roof-hiss
streaks of gold on a floor,
kinked at the door.

A cock calls the gull:
high wings play on a day of linking.

THE OLIVE THRUSH
(For Michele Magwood)

The dark of the Thrush
begins music
held in dew and joy.
Grass glitters of the moon things:
a hop,
a flit,
tseeeeep-light.

Daytime on the Thrush
in the way that butterflies are noon.

And then the suburb shouts.

THE FEW

(For Graham Warsop)

There are birds without wings in our sky,
and wings on birds that lie.
There are thoughts without dreams
and colours linked to screams.
There are some who teach but never make
below clouds we need to reach and brake.
There are reflections of opportunity
in the music of the deaf:
feathers on the air,
drummers of breath.

Blow a fluttered breeze;
tinkle the soft tips of trees,
and then run, and chase, and dance, and fly
on the wild hunt for excellence.

NIGHT FOR TIME

I have a friend who runs across continents;
one day he will run across the dark side of the sky,
at the place of moon bends and the birdless.
And at the starry times for dreamy eyes and hopes,
the pause will bring the unique tomorrow.

A path is a life;
a crack of light in the curve of moving doors and
    walls.
Hot,
fresh,
in the leak of it all.

COMMON (EUROPEAN) STARLING

Sharp spots click the buzz on wired streets;
noisy shine shits foreign aberrations and
windscreen stains.

Bougainvillea screams
different red to our *veld*;
foundling ripped from the curb;
all dizzy language of barren thorns,
stillborn on a wilderness of metal horns.

New wings and new leaves
(and plastic things made in China)
are a lie on the streets of Africa.

African Fish-Eagle

Wide river bends a Horizon Tree,
Black screams of protected sanctuary.
Water-feathers keep a course meanderingly,
Steady, soaring for the sea.

Bubbles stink on smiles excrementally
About a leaking sore from a septic knee.
Low fumes and quiet farms of family
Curve softly into veins of humanity.

And there, coming from a cut in the skies,
Hook of speed,
In dripping feed.

Quiet: the mamba-blink of the butterfly.

SEA GULL

(For Jenny Crwys-Williams)

Adrift above a cloth of sequins,
The dressmaker works.
Stitching the Pristine,
Black above, white below,
Cutting in between.
A cry of thought in feathers of froth,
A green wave is tossed.
And glass jewels sprinkle the sand.
Down she comes, alone, to think.
A wing, a gentle hand;
A line of lace, a place:
Arniston: Gown of Overberg.

POETS

Why do some poets   hop
Their words around a page,
Cheating the phrase?

The little bird: a flitting leaf,
Torn, tinkling on the branch-bounce,
Yet surely

falling.

INTERNET OF THE WORLD

Heavy, old magnet of earth,
The tortoise slides round
Like half the world.
Pink-tongued and silent in a
Handwriting of grass.

Nearby, the little sparrow
Makes a different shadow.
Free   to the wide lawn of green.

Click:

Up   into a stream
Of air,
Connecting

To almost anywhere.

LEOPARD OF YALA

(For the Cape Bird Club)

Crying in the seeing of things
Is a breaking of leaves
All green in need
All furred in speed
Bloody roadkill rolls and reeks
A city street of wildness creaks
Lost in the fumes of a butterfly scream
No chance
No space
No place
Yet the leopard speaks of
Disconnections
In a dust of crowds
How I wish we watched
Beyond our hanging shrouds
Above a metal heat
Above the dead of living feet:
A new land of Yala:
Spoorline of a new colour

RAINBOW TREE

Jewel pits near the sea
Set a land in leaves and tunnels.
Lightning sapphires pull a shore of small boats,
Moored tightly to the tide.
Poles of men fish
On a glittering day,
Leaning in a spicy heat of brown,
The *bajaj* scurries like the insect
Along tiny streets of tassel-flags,
Warm in the people of rice.
Unusual butterflies bob as peridot on
Waving hands,
Green to the click on the land
And a tree sways of colours
For wooden masks,
Of faces that make memories
And island birds.
Fields waddle in between the hills of tea;
Giant steps to the sky
Of sweet Sri Lanka:
A shadow for an owl:

Serendib of golden elephants;
Serendib of shining leopards;
Serendib, the dark glow in a rainbow,
Swaying to the *baila* of the birdwatcher.

CLOUDS FOR WORDS

(For Bridget Impey)

White clouds are reliable for rain
Like the credibility of a promise.
A flick of grey;
A shadowed fringe of thought.
Then a wise smile
Against the many hills:
Mounds made by scattering ants,
All cool in the heat of talent.
And with the flow of a linen blouse,
A soft breeze sifts
The gathered dusts from the
Mud-piled cathedrals of creativity;
And sometimes a book comes
Like the sun.

FULLSTOP

Filling the fallen nest;
Cupped, soft textured in a life;
Grasping the soiled past of moments.
Potted in broken places, spattered and holed for wild
    plants;
And circles, circles, always circles of
Twigs, tight in a snug basket of opportunity, make
Round, plated things like the food of findings,
Fresh as a hole for seed and feed;
Lying fertile in a natural pause,
ready to bloom.

And a row of words can rest before the beginning of
A new row uncurls,
Mating and minding and growing like a lifting
Bird of birdsong;
Budding either side, sentenced by a
Dot.

PENGUIN

Lying in a bed of gravity,
Horizontal moments rest
In a flatness of sleep.

Bound to the deep contours is another altitude:
The elastic emergency.

Away from us things are free and
Finned into wings and open shadows,
Like little Panda Bears on a waddling forest.

The current of time screams a dead line of crime.
Feathers and water fold fishless in a vacant
    transparency:
Bubbled skin stretches away breath and
The Ocean is a hard board bending like flypaper in
    the breeze:
The sticky illusion of life.

BULLET

Shouting a sharp curse of air
will hurt like an unnecessary hole of fear.

Our world of voids
Is a place of islands:
Dots on the sea,
Squashed of purity.
So many names lost to me.

FLOWERBIRD

Of the hills
Flutters like a national flag
Streaming tails of anthems,
Dusting our future on a soft wind of wings.

Fynbos Ruler of Hills and
Unique fingerprints of feathers and heraldic fronds,
Bridges the land to the sky.
Oh what a sprinkling of jubilation:
Like a tickertape parade of pollen
Sharing languages in a song.
Roots and vines in shadows intertwined for our
    commonality:
The sovereignty: Erica, Protea, Restio and Me.
A new Flower.
A new Bush.
A new Reed.
A new Tree.

SKYWORK

I watched a bird fly
And up there was the home of art.

One day I will paint the air,
and a canvas, filled with exquisite colours and forms,
    will float to me:
In the way clouds make thought edgeless;
In the way wind gives autumn leaves to Pointillists;
In the way rain shapes winter branches for
    Expressionists;
In the way heat shimmers landscapes at
    Abstractionists;
In the way Picasso surely watched children;
In the way breath on cold glass waits for fingers.

BODY

Wild birds of the park
Slit the day like the neck of a man,
Hopping a spattering of leaves,
Crisp in the dawn of dry dew,
Before the curl of light
Rises flies and soiled screams
towards the heart of a
terrible song.

WALKING BIRD

Long, wide pondering veld:
tussock skinned, fresh in flesh; yet blackened by the sky:
stretched tight
like a plastic garbage-bag.

Secretarybird – prancer of teary light –
drips a new rain of plumes among Coca-Cola bottles,
cereal boxes, discarded cars and cans.
It will not end the walk
until our heap is too steep.

Making Architecture

(For my Dad and Binda)

sings the form of a new thing
unlike the obligate hole
of the mouse or
the exquisite pod of the seed,
or the great dent on grass made when creatures feed.

Architecture is taking light
into bounces and original bends,
unlike the Frisbee or the spinning top,
it is not a trend.

Unlike the hint on heated hills,
or the glint through burning trees,
or the shadows under waves,
or the sparkles from caves;
we architects are not flickering-flame-watchers.
We are fire dancers.

Making architecture is a mind
that squeaks in pencil-dust and finger-feet,
giving breath to fluttered paper for a rising in your
    street.

Unlike textures on a cliff
or curved pebbles in a stream,
we architects do not wait for wind and water-work,
    instead we dream.

Making architecture is a chance to cry before
empty ridings, flapping calls,
wired windows and wired walls.
We architects are for the birds
living, lost about rare words.

GREEN STREET

The crack
The split
The gap
The life
The place between mountains

There is no street without walls

The praying hands
The squeezing thighs
The pressing bodies

There is no street without walls

The lines of leaves in a rhythm of trees
The row of shadows that breathe

The lines of leaves designed for us
The route for roots
The rush

FENCES NEAR GRAAFF-REINET

(For Mel and Simon)

Maps are yellow trees
On a green world of parchment.
Orange leaves glitter on red roofs,
Spaced like symbols and families.
Tall, blue birds and muddy sheep
Mix like wild flowers.
Sometimes Springbok shout black numbers in
Grids and gates,
Marking the latitudes and longitudes of shadows:
Rusting lines of selection,
Too sharp for reflection.
Neighbours are given to neighbours in
Tight wanderings,
Waiting for the yellow trees to
Crowd like clouds,
Gaggling in new foreign languages;
Lost from the freedom of homes;
Lost from the roaring days before fields and the old
    hills of the
Unmapped.

CROW

Face flat and
Black
In the tight space of clouds
It hit
Wide hands on
Hard slabs
Shifting blue like glue
Moving bruised in the sting of sun
In easy ways then
Rocking long on asphalt tongues of
The big new body
Whipped into convenient routes
Fast Food
The wait for
Spit

DONKEY CART ROAD

The doll's head lay like a popped cork:
Hollow plastic ball of blonde, nylon hair and
A smile.
Brain of hot sand and siftings leaked
Gravel and dust
Into a blanket
Knitted by thorns.
Nearby a little river slept
Under the shade of waddling trees.
A tossed kingfisher sparkled
Into yesterday.
And the Karoo cart came
Kicked like a toy.

KUDU HORNS ON A GATE

Swinging meat creaks
onto the sunny morning of pretty flowers.
All bloomed in the colours of a dripping Christmas.
Kicking legs and swishing tails shadow children of
    bounding fun.
Scuffed dust makes a fan of sand,
As a rusting spider web flutters like a stiff flag for
the farm and,
for the game of glory:
Floating Spoor and White Skulls.
And thorns of tinsel unwrap tomorrow:
a place of pendulous baubles, festivities and dead things.

OSTRICH

Feather dusters are long sticks that live with hands
In a dance to shadows that bends the neck of time.

People are incrementally plumed along lines of
   aspiration.
Homes shine in aging rows, polished for shows:
The great display winged from an air of ownership.

Yet settled and swaying in the sands of sanctuary,
At the address of kings and queens and flat trees, is
The biggest of all:
Castle of Africa.

CARRYING SHADOWS

in the night on the bellies of owls,
all the sirens call in our screaming vowels
at the twitching trees and sparkling lawns,
when the mountains lean on the city's yawns;
in a silent shining of a billion feet,
as the hospitals fill with our slaughtered sheep,
is to drift like foam from the waterfall,
on a quiet pool of a helpless call.

Carrying shadows are the leaves at the doors of
    mourning.
Carrying shadows are the leaves of warning,

Tiny shadows, brittle shadows, breaking shadows.

JELLYFISH BAY
(For Dr Ross Wanless and the penguins)

Cape Town floats translucently in a dead light.
Birds are gone from the night.
What shines stings.
What moves twists a current of killing.
The wobbling dawn swims in distant obligations,
lifting seagulls, adrift above the plastic sea;
and the lonely trees rise, fake and buoyant
on the concrete and the tar.

I am sleeping in a mess: a scar,
coiled for tomorrow.

Dawn Chorus

(For Mark Anderson)

ON THE NIGHT: *a flat sun of shining chintz*
   shimmers:

There is something about a troupe of children, tight on
   a stage of curtains.

There is something about the stir of the unseen.

There is something about the excitement of their night.

There is something about the children of the thespian
   sky.

There is something about the children and the shifting,
   little feet.

There is something about the waving line of light.

There is something about these children that stands
   bigger than the play:

the day:

the birdsong.

FAILING IN A TOWN OF HIGH MOUNTAINS

Is falling against an immediate wall of words
That reads as a short list of others,
Made to sentence me
To a new happiness:
The alphabetical place of rules;
The order of jewels;
The shining, plastic necklace of pop:
The cheap, political shop.

The newspaper drop:

What sells sells;
What shines is goldish gold

Homes are about seeing not about views:
A place to search for birds
In a garden of hapless hews.

TREES

(For Tykie and Vlad)

Are mountains and seas, and a
homemaker's keys.

I do not need the heat on the edge of cities: the
    shimmer and the shame.
I do not need the peaks up near the stars: the
    reaching, the taking, the blame-game.
I do not want the bends of Earth that curl like the
    hardest dreams:
the steel water or the steel land;
the tight slit of faraway; the slamming vastness of
    another lonely day.

Just give me a tree.

I do not need the bright windows onto Clifton Bay
or the wide porches framing the Milky Way.
I do not need the panorama, the diorama, or the
    dead world of distance.

Give me a tree, a real tree:

A home holds the roof of a tree like children
hold hands, and the freshness of leaves mix new
pastorals with every, single sun. Big, old branches,
swing in so many textures, they seem to hug like
bucolic, Bohemian breasts, and sometimes a bow
bends with the little skips of feet, pulling scuffs of
sand like paintings made by roots. Eaves fold into
a canopy of singing rooms extending into bark,
soft like memories. Green feelings, orange ways,
red thoughts, yellow secrets all flutter in the bright
holes of glass. And doors make moments against
the fingers of the tree, holding a home so beautifully
open and yet so together for me. And in summertime
a path of twigs always gives a family to the birds.

QUOMODOCUNQUIZING

'is making money in any way you can' (**1**).
A word of great commodity.
It occurred to me that words are powerfully rich,
laughing before the joke is written like Hadeda birds
    in our earliest sky: our *world* is a word:
a thing that can only ever be preciously read or it's
    dead.

All is for the birds anyway.

1- (Forsyth M. *The Horologicon,* published in
    the UK in 2012 by Icon Books Ltd, Omnibus
    Business Centre, probably within walking
    distance of the bank: half way down page 83,
    under the heading EARNING A LIVING).

A Life

is always someone's memory of someone else's time
the story of a pose

But sharing time unfolds a dance
the ancestral flow of heirs and air
the wind cupped and carried in new hands
the blood of bloods
the flock of shining birds – so red, so hot up high –
the place where light goes

ACKNOWLEDGEMENTS

Although my poems come from a very quiet, solitary place, their appearance in a book is a journey filled with the dedication, fellowship and kindness of a gifted team. I am deeply grateful to those who have played a part in the production of this book: Bridget Impey, Klara Skinner, Kerrie Barlow, Jenny Prangley, Megan Mance, Shawn Paikin, Shay Heydenrych, Janine Daniels and Farisai Nyaoda.

Vernon RL Head was born in 1967 in Cape Town, South Africa. He grew up in a bungalow near the sea and the gulls. He studied architecture, winning national and international awards for design and creative thinking. He is past chairman of BirdLife South Africa, one of Africa's biggest and most influential conservation organisations, and presently serves on the Advisory Board of the Percy FitzPatrick Institute of African Ornithology (UCT). He is author of the critically acclaimed bestseller *The Search for the Rarest Bird in the World*. When not writing, he is either designing special buildings or travelling the world looking for the rarest birds. This is his first collection of poetry.